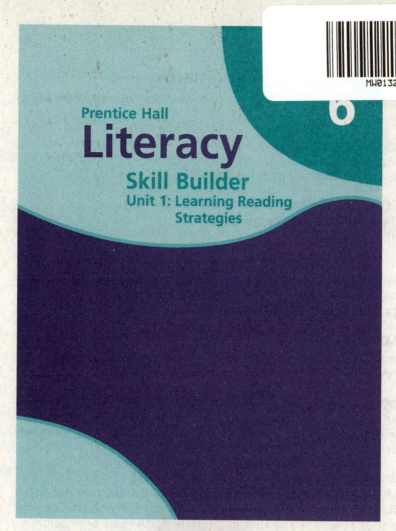

Prentice Hall
Literacy
Skill Builder
Unit 1: Learning Reading Strategies

PEARSON
Prentice Hall

Boston, Massachusetts
Upper Saddle River, New Jersey

Copyright © 2007 by Pearson Education, Inc., publishing as Pearson Prentice Hall, Boston, Massachusets 02116. All rights reserved. Printed in the United States of America. This publication is protected by copyright, and permission should be obtained from the publisher prior to any prohibited reproduction, storage in a retrieval system, or transmission in any form or by any means, electronic, mechanical, photocopying, recording, or likewise. The publisher hereby grants permission to reproduce these pages, in part or in whole, for classroom use only, the number not to exceed the number of students in each class. Notice of copyright must appear on all copies. For information regarding permission(s), write to: Rights and Permissions Department, One Lake Street, Upper Saddle River, New Jersey 07458.

Pearson Prentice Hall™ is a trademark of Pearson Education, Inc.
Pearson® is a registered trademark of Pearson plc.
Prentice Hall® is a registered trademark of Pearson Education, Inc.

ISBN 0-13-200699-5

3 4 5 6 7 8 9 10   11 10 09 08 07

Acknowledgments

Grateful acknowledgment is made to the following for copyrighted material:

Archaelogy
"Human Footprints at Chauvet Cave," by Spencer P.M. Harrington from *Archaelogy*, Volume 52, Number 5, September/October 1999. Copyright © 1999 by the Archaeological Institute of America.

G.P. Putnam's Sons, a division of Penguin Putnam Inc.
"Two Kinds" by Amy Tan from *The Joy Luck Club*. Copyright © 1989 by Amy Tan.

HarperCollins Publishers, Inc.
From *The Pigman and Me* (pp.97-100) by Paul Zindel. Copyright © 1991 by Paul Zindel. From *The Wounded Wolf* by Jean Craghead George. Text copyright © 1978 by Jean Craighead George.

Houghton Mifflin Company
"Arachne" from *Greek Myths*. Copyright © 1949 by Olivia E. Coolidge; copyright renewed © 1977 by Olivia E. Coolidge.

Lensey Namioka c/o Ruth Cohen Literary Agency, Inc.
"The All-American Slurp," by Lensey Namioka, copyright © 1987, from *Visions*, ed. By Donald R. Gallo. Reprinted by permission of Lensey Namioka. All rights reserved by the author.

Michael Courlander for the Emma Courlander Trust
"All Stories Are Anansi's" from *The Hat-Shaking Dance and Other Ashanti Tales from Ghana* by Harold Courlander with Albert Kofi Prempeh. Copyright © 1957 by Harcourt, Inc.; 1985 by Harold Courlander. Used by permission.

Ricardo E. Alegría
From "The Three Wishes" from *The Three Wishes: A Collection of Puerto Rican Folktales*, selected and adapted by Ricardo E. Alegría, translated by Elizabeth Culbert.

Pearson Education Inc.
"Populations and Communities" from Prentice Hall Science Explorer: Life Science.

University Press of New England
Gary Soto "The Drive-In Movies," from *A Summer Life* © 1990 by University Press of New England. Reprinted by permission of University Press of New England.

Note: Every effort has been made to locate the copyright owner of material reproduced on this audio component. Omissions brought to our attention will be corrected in subsequent editions.

Table of Contents

UNIT 1: Learning Reading Strategies

Section A Before You Read
- **Skill 1** Looking for Clues 4
- **Skill 2** Skimming a Passage 7
- **Skill 3** Setting a Purpose for Reading 11
- **Section A Wrap-Up** Test Prep 14
- **Section A Wrap-Up** Something Different 18

Section B While You Read
- **Skill 4** Reading First Narrative Paragraphs for Clues 19
- **Skill 5** Reading First Expository Paragraphs for Clues 21
- **Skill 6** Putting Vocabulary in Context 23
- **Skill 7** Understanding Idioms 25
- **Skill 8** Marking a Narrative Passage 28
- **Skill 9** Marking an Expository Passage 31
- **Skill 10** Taking Notes 33
- **Skill 11** Identifying the Main Idea and Supporting Details .. 35
- **Skill 12** Connecting to What You Read 38
- **Skill 13** Making Inferences from Narrative Passages 40
- **Skill 14** Making Inferences from Expository Passages 42
- **Skill 15** Making Predictions 44
- **Skill 16** Visualizing What You Read 46
- **Section B Wrap-Up** Test Prep 48
- **Section B Wrap-Up** Something Different 52

Section C After You Read
- **Skill 17** Scanning a Passage 53
- **Skill 18** Summarizing 55
- **Skill 19** Asking Questions 57
- **Skill 20** Drawing Conclusions 59
- **Section C Wrap-Up** Test Prep 61
- **Section C Wrap-Up** Something Different 64

SKILL 1: LOOKING FOR CLUES

STOP! Don't read the passage! First, ask yourself, "What can I learn from the following clues?"

- Title
- Headings
- Bold and italicized words
- Pictures and graphics

You will read narrative and expository passages. A **narrative** passage tells a story. An **expository** passage provides factual information. As you look for clues, identify the type of passage you are reading.

GUIDED PRACTICE

All Stories Are Anansi's
by Harold Courlander

Introduction: "All Stories Are Anansi's" is a trickster tale. Typically, the trickster is an animal character, such as a spider, fox, or coyote, that tries to fool others. In some tales, he succeeds. In others, he, himself, is fooled. In African folktales, of which this story is one, the trickster tries to take advantage of larger and stronger animals through cunning or magic.

See how a student interpreted the clues from the passage.
What can these clues tell you before you read the passage?

Clues	Student Interpretations
Title	The title suggests that Anansi is a storyteller or that Anansi is somehow in every story.
Italicized words	A trickster is an animal that tries to fool others.
Picture	The passage is about a spider.

Now, see if you can answer the following question based on the students interpretation of the clues. **Is the passage telling a story or providing factual information?**

_____

_____

NAME _____ DATE _____

NOW YOU TRY IT!

Two Kinds
by Amy Tan

Introduction: The mother in this story has dreams of greatness for her daughter, that her daughter feels she cannot fulfill. The mother believes there are only two kinds of daughters: the kind of daughter who obeys and the kind of daughter who disobeys.

Clues	Your Interpretation
Title	
Italicized words	
Picture	

Is the passage telling a story or providing factual information?

_____
_____
_____
_____

© by Pearson Education, Inc., publishing as Pearson Prentice Hall

Let's see how you do finding clues in a different kind of passage.

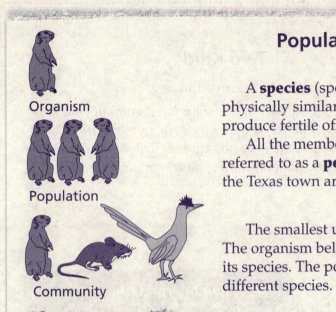

Populations and Communities

Populations
A **species** (spee sheez) is a group of organisms that are physically similar and can reproduce with each other to produce fertile offspring.

All the members of one species in a particular area are referred to as a **population**. The 400 million prairie dogs in the Texas town are one example of a population.

Communities
The smallest unit of organization is a single **organism**. The organism belongs to a **population** of other members of its species. The population belongs to a **community** of different species.

What can these clues tell you before you read the passage?

Clues	Your Interpretation
Title	
Headings	
Bold Words	
Graphic	

Is the passage telling a story or providing factual information?

_____

_____

NAME .... DATE ....

SKILL 2: SKIMMING A PASSAGE

You can improve your understanding of what you read by first skimming the passage to preview what you are about to read. **Skimming** is reading only parts of the passage to get an overall idea about the major points.

How to Skim: Read the first and last paragraphs and the first sentence of every other paragraph.

GUIDED PRACTICE

Read the highlighted words to understand the experience of skimming. The indented text summarizes the passage events and details. The rest of the text is the author's actual words.

From "The Drive-In Movies"
by Gary Soto

Introduction: If the narrator's mom was happy on a Saturday morning, she would sometimes take the narrator, his brother, and his sister to a drive-in movie. This particular Saturday the narrator does his best to make sure his mom stays in a good mood.

One Saturday I decided to be extra good. When she came out of the bedroom tying her robe, she yawned a hat-sized yawn and blinked red eyes at the weak brew of coffee I had fixed for her. I made her toast with strawberry jam spread to all the corners and set the three boxes of cereal in front of her. If she didn't care to eat cereal, she could always look at the back of the boxes as she drank her coffee.

❖ ❖ ❖

The author goes outside to pull weeds from the flower garden. Then he mows the lawn.

❖ ❖ ❖

This job was less dull because as I pushed the mower over the shaggy lawn, I could see it looked tidier. My brother and sister watched from the window. Their faces were fat with cereal, a third helping. I made a face at them when they asked how come I was working. Rick pointed to a part of the lawn. "You missed some over there." I ignored him and kept my attention on the windmill of grassy blades.

❖ ❖ ❖

A bee stings the author's foot. He almost cries. Instead, he pulls out the stinger and continues to work.

❖ ❖ ❖

I swept the front steps, took out the garbage, cleaned the lint filter of the dryer (easy), plucked hair from the industrial wash basin in the garage (also easy), hosed off the patio, smashed three snails sucking paint from the house (disgusting, but fun), tied a bundle of newspapers, put away toys, and finally, seeing that almost everything else was done and the sun was not too high, started waxing the car.

❖ ❖ ❖

His brother comes out to help. Together they wax the chrome parts of the car. Then they start waxing the paint. They use up the entire bottle of wax on half of the car. There was not enough to finish. The boys decide that half is better than nothing. They go outside for lunch. After lunch, they go back outside.

❖ ❖ ❖

Rick and I nearly jumped. The waxed side of the car was foggy white. We took a rag and began to polish vigorously and nearly in tears, but the fog wouldn't come off. I blamed Rick and he blamed me. . . Now, not only would we not go to the movies, but Mom would surely snap a branch from the plum tree and chase us around the yard.

Mom came out and looked at us with her hands on her aproned hips. Finally, she said, "You boys worked so hard." She turned on the garden hose and washed the car. That night we did go to the drive-in. The first feature was about nothing, and the second feature, starring Jerry Lewis, was *Cinderfella*. I tried to stay awake. I kept a wad of homemade popcorn in my cheek and laughed when Jerry Lewis fit golf tees in his nose. I rubbed my watery eyes. I laughed and looked at my mom. I promised myself I would remember that scene with the golf tees and promised myself not to work so hard the coming Saturday. Twenty minutes into the movie, I fell asleep with one hand in the popcorn.

Now, see how one student answered a question about the passage. Can you answer the question that follows?

What do you know about this passage so far?

It is a story about how the narrator and his brother help out around the house so they can go to the movies.

When you read the entire passage what other information should you look for?

_____

_____

NOW YOU TRY IT!

How to skim: Read the first and last paragraphs and the first sentence of the middle paragraph.

From "Human Footprints at Chauvet Cave"

by Spencer P.M. Harrington

Introduction: The writer tells about a recent discovery of human footprints in a French cave in France. The footprints might have belonged to an eight-year-old boy.

Recent exploration of the Chauvet Cave near Vallon-Pont-d'Arc in southern France has yielded the oldest footprints of <u>Homo sapiens</u> and a cavern with a dozen new animal figures. The footprints appear to be those of an eight-year-old boy, according to prehistorian Michel-Alain Garcia of the Centre National de la Recherche Scientifique, Nanterre. They are between 20 and 30 thousand years old, perhaps twice as old as those discovered previously at Aldene, Monstespan, Niaux, Pech Merle, and other Upper <u>Palaeolithic</u> sites.

Garcia estimates that the boy was about four-and-a-half feet tall, his feet more than eight inches long and three-and-a-half inches wide. First spotted in 1994 by Jean-Marie Chauvet, the cave's discoverer, the footprints stretch perhaps 150 feet and at times cross those of bears and wolves. The prints lead to the so-called room of skulls, where a number of bear skulls have been found. In a few places, there is evidence that the boy slipped on the soft clay floor, though Garcia says the prints show the boy was not running, but walking normally. The boy appears at one point to have stopped to clean his torch, charcoal from which has been dated to circa 26,000 years ago. The prints from the Chauvet Cave, like nearly all footprints thus far discovered in Palaeolithic caves, are from bare feet, which has led scholars to speculate that people of the time either left footwear at cave entrances or carried it.

Meanwhile, a team of 15 specialists directed by French prehistorian Jean Clottes recently investigated an uninventoried room originally discovered by Chauvet. There they found a dozen new paintings of mammoth, bison, and horses, among other animals. Clottes' team has so far documented 447 animals of 14 different species. By comparison, Niaux Cave in the French Pyrenees, cited by the French Palaeolithic specialist Abbé Breuil as one of the half-dozen great caves containing prehistoric art, has 110 images of six species.

> **VOCABULARY**
>
> **Homo sapiens**
> (HO mo SAY pee ens)
> *n.* modern human beings
>
> **Palaeolithic**
> (pay lee o LITH ik)
> *n.* earlierst period of the Stone Age

© by Pearson Education, Inc., publishing as Pearson Prentice Hall

What do you know about this passage so far?

_____
_____
_____
_____

When you read the entire passage what other information should you look for?

_____
_____
_____
_____

Where would you imagine finding this passage (a novel, a magazine, a newspaper, a textbook, etc.)?

_____

SETTING A PURPOSE FOR READING

You **set a purpose for reading** before you begin to read a text. Setting a purpose for reading means to decide on a reason to read a certain text. Having a reason for reading is like taking aim at a target. A purpose gives you a direction which helps you stay focused as you read.

First, use the reading strategy "Looking for Clues" to help you set a purpose for reading.

What can you learn from the title, headings, bold and italicized words, and pictures and graphics?

Next, ask yourself, "What facts and details should I look for as I read the passage?"

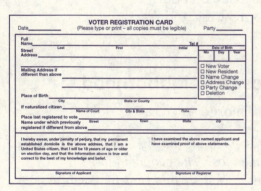

Granddaddy's Gift

by Margaree King Mitchell

Introduction: In this story, a girl named Little Joe lives in Mississippi in a time of segregation. Her grandfather is determined to become the first African American to register to vote in their rural town. He eventually succeeds, despite the opposition of the town clerk and other residents. When Little Joe turns 18, she registers simply by filling out a voter registration card.

GUIDED PRACTICE

See how a student used the clues to help her figure out what the reading was about.

Clues	Topics
Title	The story is about a gift given to Granddaddy.
Italicized words	Seems like the gift might be his voter registration card.
Picture	The picture is of a voter registration card. This makes it seem like "Granddaddy's Gift" is a voter registration card.

© by Pearson Education, Inc., publishing as Pearson Prentice Hall

What is the purpose for reading this passage? ?

My purpose for reading is to learn why Little Joe's grandfather had a hard time registering to vote. I would like to find out why Little Joe's experience with voting is so different from her grandfather's experience. I will read to find out what gift Little Joe received from her grandfather.

What facts and details should this student look for as he reads the passage?

_____

_____

NOW YOU TRY IT!

Fill in the chart. First, look for clues to figure out what the essay is about. Then, use the information in the chart to set a purpose for reading and write your purpose in the space provided.

Barrio: José's Neighborhood
by George Ancona

Introduction: This story is about the mostly Latino San Francisco neighborhood of a boy named José. The people in José's neighborhood speak Spanish, English, and sometimes Chinese. Large murals, or paintings, on the walls tell the stories of the people who live there. Festivities such as Carnaval and Day of the Dead highlight traditional Latino celebrations.

Clues	Topics
Title	
Italicized words	
Picture	

NAME _____ DATE _____

What is the purpose for reading this passage?

_____

_____

_____

What facts and details should you look for as you read the passage?

_____

_____

_____

_____

For what purpose might you read the following passage? What facts and details would you expect to find in the text?

Car repair manual _____

Movie review _____

Menu _____

Job advertisement _____

© by Pearson Education, Inc., publishing as Pearson Prentice Hall

NAME

Test Prep

Directions: Do not read all of the passage below! Instead, let's see how much information you can gather by using the pre-reading strategies you have learned. Remember that the indented words summarize the passage events and details and the author's actual words are not indented.

From "The Pigman & Me"
by Paul Zindel

Introduction: Different places have different rules. Sometimes the rules are written out for you on signs or as instructions. At other times, rules are unwritten, such as not cutting in front of people in line. Unwritten rules can be as important as written rules, as the narrator Paul Zindel finds out.

When trouble came to me, it didn't involve anybody I thought it would. It involved the nice, normal, smart boy by the name of John Quinn. Life does that to us a lot. Just when we think something awful's going to happen one way, it throws you a curve and the something awful happens another way. This happened on the first Friday, during gym period, when we were allowed to play games in the school yard.

✦ ✦ ✦

> A boy called Richard Cahill invites Paul to play paddleball with him. Richard doesn't think to tell Paul that you can only sign out the paddle for fifteen minutes at a time. When Richard goes to get a drink of water, John Quinn asks Paul for the paddle. Paul says "no." He is afraid other kids will try to take advantage of him because he is the new kid.

✦ ✦ ✦

"Look, you have to give it to me," John Quinn insisted.

That was when I did something <u>berserk</u>. I was so wound up and frightened that I didn't think, and I struck out at him with my right fist. I had forgotten I was holding the paddle, and it smacked into his face, giving him an instant black eye. John was shocked. I was shocked. Richard Cahill came running back and he was shocked.

VOCABULARY

berserk (ber ZERK) *adj.*
in a violent frenzy

✦ ✦ ✦

> John complains to Mr. Trellis, the gym teacher. Paul says that John tried to take the paddle away from him. Mr. Trellis explains the rules to Paul.

✦ ✦ ✦

"I'm sorry," I said, over and over again.

Then the bell rang, and all John Quinn whispered to me was that he was going to get even.

✦ ✦ ✦

John announces that he is going to take revenge on Paul after school on Monday. Paul is scared because he has never been in a fight.

Paul tells Nonno Frankie, his grandfather, what happened. Nonno Frankie says he will teach Paul everything about Italian fighting, He says Paul will be able to smack John Quinn around like pizza dough.

◆ ◆ ◆

Nonno Frankie suddenly let out a yell. "Aaeeeeeyaaaayeeeeeh!" It was so blood-curdlingly weird. I decided to wait until he felt like explaining it.

◆ ◆ ◆

Nonno Frankie yells again. He says it is good to yell like this because it confuses your enemy.

◆ ◆ ◆

"Is that all I need to know?" I asked, now more afraid than ever of facing John Quinn in front of all the kids. . . "But how do I hold my hands to fight? How do I hold my fists?" I wanted to know.

"Like this!" Nonno Frankie demonstrated, taking a boxing stance with his left foot and fist forward.

"And then I just swing my right fist forward as hard as I can?"

"No. First you curse him."

◆ ◆ ◆

Nonno Frankie gives Paul a list of curses to use, ending with "an espresso coffee cup would fit on his head like a sombrero."

◆ ◆ ◆

"And then you just give him the big Sicilian surprise!"

"What?"

"You kick him in the shins!"

◆ ◆ ◆

By the time Monday morning comes, Paul is very nervous. Nonno Frankie has gone back to New York. Paul's mother and sister don't say anything, so Paul assumes they haven't heard about the fight.

◆ ◆ ◆

In every class I went to, it seemed there were a dozen different kids coming over to me and telling me they heard John Quinn was going to beat me up after school.

◆ ◆ ◆

At 3 P.M., the bell rings, and the kids start leaving school. Paul stays behind, cleaning his desk and taking time to pack up his books. Finally, he leaves the building, with Jennifer, his friend, at his side. In the field across the street, John Quinn and a huge crowd of kids are waiting. Jennifer tells Paul that he could run, but he refuses.

◆ ◆ ◆

John stood with his black eye, and his fists up.

I stopped a few feet from him and put my fists up. A lot of kids in the crowd started to shout, "Kill him, Johnny!" but I may have imagined that part.

◆ ◆ ◆

John and Paul both dance like fighters. Most of the crowd wants the fight to begin, but Jennifer tries to talk the boys out of it.

◆ ◆ ◆

But John came in for the kill. He was close enough now so any punch he threw could hit me. All I thought of was Nonno Frankie, but I couldn't remember half of what he told me and I didn't think any of it would work anyway.

"Aaeeeeeyaaaayeeeeeh!" I suddenly screamed at John. He stopped in his tracks and the crowd froze in amazed silence. Instantly, I brought back my right foot, and shot it forward to kick John in his left shin.

◆ ◆ ◆

The crowd is shocked and boos Paul. He misses John's shin and kicks again. Meanwhile, John throws a punch at Paul. It barely touches him, but he is so busy kicking that he trips and falls down. The crowd cheers, believing it was John's punch that knocked Paul down.

◆ ◆ ◆

I decided to go along with it. I <u>groveled</u> in the dirt for a few moments, and then stood up slowly holding my head as if I'd received a death blow. John put his fists down. He was satisfied justice had been done and his black eye had been avenged.

◆ ◆ ◆

John turns to leave. But a boy called Moose complains that John didn't punch Paul enough. John says it's over, but Moose says it's not. As Moose moves closer to Paul, a girl with long blond hair suddenly strikes Moose from behind. She has her hands around his neck, choking him. Then she lets go, throwing Moose about ten feet. Paul sees that it's his sister! She gives a stern warning to anyone who might try to hurt her brother again. Moose is not happy, but the crowd breaks up and heads home.

◆ ◆ ◆

I guess that was the first day everybody learned that, if nothing else, the Zindel kids stick together. As for Nonno Frankie's Sicilian fighting <u>technique</u>, I came to realize he was ahead of his time. In fact, these days it's called karate.

VOCABULARY

groveled (GROV eld)
v. lay or crawled about before someone in hope of mercy

technique (tek NEEK)
n. method

NAME _____ DATE _____

Answer the questions below.

LOOKING FOR CLUES

What can these clues tell you before you read the passage?

Title

_____

_____

Italicized Words

_____

_____

Pictures

_____

_____

SKIMMING THE TEXT

What do you know about the passage so far?

_____

_____

_____

SETTING A PURPOSE FOR READING

What do you want to find out from reading the passage?

_____

_____

Something Different...
WHAT'S THE POINT?

You may ask that question a lot, especially about chores you do not like to do. The question really asks "What is the purpose?" Often when you know the purpose, or goal, of the chore it easier to do it well. Sometimes you can make the chore more fun if you set a different purpose.

Work together in groups to write a list of different chores that group members do. Then, think about what the true purpose is of each chore. Next think of a different purpose you could set to make the chore more fun.

Example:

Chore: **Doing the dishes**

Purpose 1: **to help your family; to keep the house clean; to keep you and your family from getting sick**

Purpose 2: **to save the dinner dishes from a suffocating death by the spicy garlic sauce your mom made**

Chore: _____
_____

Purpose 1: _____

Purpose 2: _____

Chore: _____
_____

Purpose 1: _____

Purpose 2: _____

Chore: _____
_____

Purpose 1: _____

Purpose 2: _____

NAME _____ DATE _____

SKILL 4: READING FIRST NARRATIVE PARAGRAPH FOR CLUES

The first paragraph of a **narrative**, a written story, introduces character(s), setting, and plot. Use the first paragraph to gather clues about the narrative before you read the entire passage.

GUIDED PRACTICE

See how the student used the information from the chart to answer the following questions.

> In January, a puppy wandered onto the property of Mr. Amos Lacey and his wife, Mamie, and their daughter, Doris. Icicles hung three feet or more from the eaves of houses, snowdrifts swallowed up automobiles, and the birds were so fluffed up they looked comical.

From reading the first paragraph of this narrative, the student gathered the following details.

Elements of Narrative	Details from the First Paragraph
Characters	• a puppy • Mamie • Mr. Amos Lacey • Doris
Setting	the Laceys' home "Icicles hung" "snowdrifts swallowed up automobiles" "birds were . . . fluffed up"
Plot	"puppy wandered onto the [Laceys'] property"

See how the student used the information from the chart to answer the following questions.

From reading the first paragraph, the student made the following logical guesses.
- Named characters are important.
- The puppy seems to be an important character, because the paragraph tells you the conditions the puppy has to deal with.

From reading the first paragraph, the student expects the narrative will answer the following question.
- Will the Laceys find the puppy?

Review the student responses on page 19 and answer the questions below.

What other questions do you expect the narrative to answer?

_____

_____

NOW YOU TRY IT!

Now see what information you can gather from the clues presented in this first paragraph.

> Once upon a time, when wishes were aplenty, a fisherman and his wife lived by the side of the sea. All that they ate came out of the sea. Their hut was covered with the finest mosses that kept them cool in the summer and warm in the winter. And there was nothing they needed or wanted except a child.

From reading this first paragraph of this narrative, you know the following details.

Elements of Narrative	Details from the First Paragraph
Character(s)	
Setting	
Plot	

From reading the first paragraph, what logical guesses can you make about the narrative?

_____

_____

From reading the first paragraph, what questions would you expect the narrative to answer?

_____

_____

NAME _____ DATE _____

SKILL 5: READING FIRST EXPOSITORY PARAGRAPHS FOR CLUES

The first paragraph of an **expository** passage, a reading that explains something, introduces the main idea and some of the supporting ideas of the passage.

GUIDED PRACTICE

See how a student gathered information from the first paragraph of the expository passage.

> For thousands of years, humans had tried to fly. And although every attempt failed, that did not stop people from trying. Watching birds fly made humans long for the freedom of flight. Then, during the fifteenth century, Leonardo da Vinci turned to the study of flight. Like many before him, Leonardo based his ideas on the wings of birds. He made drawings of flying machines with bird-like flapping wings. However, none of them ever got off the ground.

From reading the first paragraph, the student gathered the following details.

Elements of Expository Passages	Details from the First Paragraph
Main Idea	For thousands of years people tried to fly
Supporting Ideas	Leonardo da Vinci tried to develop flying machines, but none ever got off the ground

See how the student used the information from the chart to answer the following questions.

From reading the first paragraph, the student made the following logical guesses about the expository passage.

- The author knows that people have tried to learn how to fly.
- Da Vinci produced drawings of many machines, but his flying machines did not work.

Review the student responses and answer the question below.

From reading the first paragraph, what questions would you expect the expository passage to answer?

_____

_____

© by Pearson Education, Inc., publishing as Pearson Prentice Hall

NOW YOU TRY IT!

Now see what information you can gather from the clues presented in this first paragraph.

> In Greek mythology, the Gorgons were three sisters who had wings. Two of the Gorgons, Stheno and Euryale, were immortal, while, the third, Medusa, was mortal. These sisters had all been beautiful at one time but were changed into hideous monsters with snakes in place of hair. They also had very long tongues and huge teeth. Their stare turned anyone who saw them into stone.

From reading this first paragraph of this expository passage, you know the following details.

Elements of Expository Passages	Details from the First Paragraph
Main Idea	
Supporting Ideas	

From reading the first paragraph, what logical guesses can you make about the expository passage?

_____

_____

_____

From reading the first paragraph, what questions would you expect the expository passage to answer?

_____

_____

_____

NAME .... DATE ....

SKILL 6: PUTTING VOCABULARY IN CONTEXT

Readers experience unfamiliar words all the time. Knowing how to put vocabulary in context is an important strategy for all readers. A word's **context** is made up of the words and phrases that appear around or near that word, and that help to specify its meaning.

GUIDED PRACTICE

Let's look at how one student figured out the word's meaning by finding the context clues in the sentence and the sentence that follows it.

> The rain continued to **hamper** Jack's progress. He was becoming more frustrated as he kept slipping backward down the hill.

Can you figure out what the word in the bold type means?

Word	Context Clues
hamper	one

Now see how the student figures out what the context clues tell her about the word.

1. Progress is what Jack wants to accomplish.
2. Slipping shows that Jack is not making progress.
3. Frustrated describes how Jack feels.
   He feels frustrated because he is not making progress.
   Hamper must mean to hinder or slow down because it Jack is frustrated by his lack of progress.

See if you can figure out the definition based on the clues gathered by the student.

Hamper means: _____

_____

Now go back and reread the sentence. Does that definition make sense?

_____

© by Pearson Education, Inc., publishing as Pearson Prentice Hall

Note: some words have more than one meaning. Several of the answers below are definitions for the word channel, but not in the context of the sentence.

NOW YOU TRY IT!

See if you can answer the multiple-choice question that follows the passage.

> I've piloted this boat so many times that I could find the *channel* blindfolded. My folks have let me steer since I was ten. Now I know what to look for even when the river's water is muddy and brown. A rock on the east bank, a dead tree on the west bank, and the sandbar under the cliffs—these landmarks help me find my way.

In this passage, the word *channel* means
   A. a particular television station.
   B. a deeper part of a river.
   C. to make a groove in.
   D. a metal bar with a bracket-shaped section.

Word	Context Clues
Channel	

Explain what the context clues tell you about the word.
_____
_____

What does *channel* mean?
_____
_____

Now go back and reread the passage. Does that definition make sense?
_____
_____

Understanding Idioms

In your reading, when you encounter an expression that you don't understand, it may be an **idiom**. An idiom is a saying or expression that is descriptive but cannot be understood from the literal meaning, or dictionary definition, of its individual words.

GUIDED PRACTICE

Read the passage. Can you figure out what the idiom **"in stitches"** means?

> I think our entire family showed up to see Suzanne in the school play. We had heard that it was a funny play. I could barely see because Grandpa sat in front of me. As the play continued, he and Grandma kept laughing. Mom, sitting beside me, pointed at them and said, "They've been **in stitches** the entire play!"

What would a representation of the literal meaning of "in stitches" look like? Draw it below.	What does the idiom "in stitches" describe? Draw it below.

© by Pearson Education, Inc., publishing as Pearson Prentice Hall

Let's look at how one student figured out the idiom's meaning by finding the context clues in the sentence and the sentences that comes before it.

Idiom	Context Clues
"in stitches"	"We had heard that it was a funny play" "He and Grandma kept laughing"

Now see how the student figures out what the context clues tell her about the idiom.

> "We had heard that it was a funny play" provides a clue why Grandma and Grandpa are laughing.
>
> "He and Grandma kept laughing" is followed by Mom's statement that they've been laughing during the play.

See if you can figure out what the idiom means based on the information the student gathered.

"In stitches" means

_____

_____

Go back and read the paragraph. Does your definition make sense?

_____

NOW YOU TRY IT!

Can you figure out what the idiom **"face the music"** means by looking at the context clues in the passage below?

> For the third day in a row, Gene had not done his homework. Ms. Turner accepted his excuse the first day. The next day she said he could turn it in late, but with ten points off. On the way to school today, I told Gene that Ms. Turner wouldn't let him off this time. He would have to **face the music**.

NAME _____   DATE _____

| What would a representation of the literal meaning of "face the music" look like? Draw it below. | In the previous paragraph, what does "face the music" describe? Draw it below. |

Idiom	Context Clues
"face the music"	

What do the context clues tell you about the idiom?

_____

_____

What does "face the music" mean?

_____

_____

Go back and reread the passage. Does that definition make sense?

_____

_____

© by Pearson Education, Inc., publishing as Pearson Prentice Hall

SKILL 8: MARKING A NARRATIVE PASSAGE

Marking the passage is a great strategy for staying focused and will help you note important information as you read. How you mark the passage depends upon the kind of passage it is. Here is how to mark a narrative passage.

How to Mark the Text	What the Mark Means
Circle character (names)	Identifies a character.
Underline descriptive details	Identifies important details about the character(s) and setting.
1, 2, 3, . . .	Identifies the sequence of events of the plot.
Underline twice	Identifies the conflict.
Put ? in the margin, and [ ] bracket the text	Identifies sections of the text that are confusing and that you can return to later.

GUIDED PRACTICE

Look at the following passage to see how one student marked the text.

> (Arachne) a young Greek woman. Arachne was not rich or famous or beautiful. She came from a small village where her father was known for his ability to dye, or color, wool into beautiful colors. But Arachne was more talented than her father. [1]She spun the wool into soft thread and then wove it into beautiful cloth on a loom.
>
> [2]People came from far away to watch her. They said that the goddess (Athene) must have taught Arachne her great skill. But Arachne was very proud and did not like people to think she learned her skill from anyone else, even from a goddess. She told them that Athene herself could not weave cloth more beautiful than her own.

Now see if you can answer the following question only by looking at the parts of the passage the student marked.

How did Arachne learn her skill?

_____

_____

NOW YOU TRY IT!

Mark the text as you read.

The Three Wishes

by Ricardo E. Algria

Long ago, a woodsman and his wife lived in a small house in the forest. They were poor but happy. And they always shared what they had with others. One day while the husband was working far away in the forest, an old man came to the house. He was lost and hungry. The wife gave him something to eat. After he ate, the old man said he would reward her for her kindness.

The old man answered, "Beginning immediately, any three wishes you or your husband may wish will come true."

When she heard these words, the woman was overjoyed and exclaimed, "Oh, if my husband were only here to hear what you say!"

The last words had scarcely left her lips when the woodsman appeared in the little house with the ax still in his hands. The first wish had come true.

His wife hugged him happily and told him what had happened. The husband, without thinking, became angry with his wife for wasting one of the wishes. He had never been angry with her before. His greed made him yell at her. He told her she was stupid and wished that she would grow donkey ears. And she did. When she felt her ears, she began to cry. Her husband was sorry and ran to comfort her.

The old man, who had stood by silently, now came to them and said, "Until now, you have known happiness together and have never quarreled with each other. Nevertheless, the mere knowledge that you could have riches and power has changed you both. Remember, you have only one wish left. What do you want? Riches? Beautiful clothes? Servants? Power?"

The woodsman tightened his arm about his wife, looked at the man, and said, "We want only the happiness and joy we knew before my wife grew donkey's ears."

What did you mark? (Notice that you do not need to reread the passage. All you do is refer to the markings to retrieve information.)

Narrative Elements	What You Marked
Characters	
Descriptive details	
Sequence of events of the plot	
Conflict	

Marking an Expository Passage

Marking the passage can keep you stay focused as you read. Here is how to **mark an expository passage**.

How to Mark the Text	What the Mark Means
Circle character (names)	Identifies the topic or topics of the passage.
Underline twice	Identifies the important details that support the important ideas.
Underline once	
Put ? in the margin, and [bracket the text]	Identifies sections of the text that are confusing and that you can return to later or research further.

GUIDED PRACTICE

Look at the following passage to see how one student marked an expository passage.

> *One crow for sorrow, Two crows for mirth . . .*
> So begins an old counting rhyme that reflects the ways in which the crow is viewed in folklore. (The crow has been both feared and admired since ancient times.)
> ? The crow belongs to a family of birds that includes the raven and the magpie. They are *carrion* birds, meaning they eat dead flesh. Crows, in fact, will eat anything. Crows will also band together to steal another animal's meal. However, they rarely steal from each other.
> In folklore, the crow is often an omen of death, probably because of its color and carrion diet. This is the dark side of the "trickster" crow. In one fable, however, a vain crow [is itself tricked by flattery]. ?

See if you can answer the following question, by looking at just the parts of the text that the student marked.

Why is the crow often an omen of death?

_____

_____

_____

© by Pearson Education, Inc., publishing as Pearson Prentice Hall   31

NOW YOU TRY IT!

Mark the text as you read.

> Have you ever watched the rain hitting the windowpane, the droplets clinging to the glass and running down the smooth surface? Did you know that each droplet of rainwater is the same water that has fallen as rain throughout time? This process is called the water cycle. Nearly all of the Earth's water passes through the water cycle over and over again. The amount of water that has been created or lost during the past billion years is very small.
>
> Here is how the water cycle works. After a rainfall, the sun comes out, and the heat from its rays hits the Earth. The puddles of water dry up and turn into water vapor, which rises into the air. The coolness of the higher air causes the water vapor to turn back into water droplets. The droplets collect into clouds, which then drop the water back to Earth during the next rainstorm. The same water that was in the puddle will again fall to Earth. Then the water cycle is ready to begin again.

What did you mark? Complete the chart below. Note that you do not need to reread the whole passage. Just read what you marked.

Expository Elements	What You Marked
Topics	
Important ideas	
Important details	

SKILL 10

TAKING NOTES

Taking notes helps you keep track of key facts and ideas. Notes help you to remember or know where to search for the facts and ideas at a later time. Reading your notes is faster than rereading a passage. When you take notes, you paraphrase what the passage states. **Paraphrase** means to restate something in your own words.

When you take notes on a piece of paper, organize your notes like this:

1. Number the most important ideas.
    A. Indent and letter the facts or details that relate to the idea above.
        1. Repeat as many times as needed.
            b. Indent each time an idea or detail relates to the one before.

2. Do not indent new ideas.
    B. Remember that indenting correctly clarifies the relationships between the ideas and details.

GUIDED PRACTICE

See how one student took notes without copying the text word for word. She paraphrased the most important ideas and details. Try to fill in the missing notes

> The roots of many of our freedoms can be traced to an unpopular king. John had become king of England in 1199. John almost lost his power by angering many of England's nobles. He lost a series of expensive wars with France. When John demanded heavy taxes from the nobles, many refused to pay. They also threatened to rebel unless John agreed to a long list of demands.
>
> That list was the Magna Carta (Latin for "Great Charter"). The nobles wrote it to limit John's powers and to protect their rights. The Magna Carta included such concepts as trial by jury, freedom from heavy taxes, church freedom, and due process of law. Many rights included in the Magna Carta, such as trial by jury, were adopted by the United States.

1. The Magna Carta was created to limit King John's powers
    A. it was originally intended to protect nobles
    B. _____
    C. The Magna Carta included many important concepts
        1. _____
        2. _____
        3. trial by jury
            a. _____

NOW YOU TRY IT!

Take notes on the lines provided as you read. Remember to paraphrase only the most important ideas and details.

> Do blood-sucking bats really exist? Yes—in Central and South America. Most bats survive by speeding through the air and catching small insects. Vampire bats, on the other hand, drink blood. In fact, they are the only known mammals that survive solely by drinking blood.
>
> So how do they get blood? Vampire bats have small, sharp teeth that they use to make a small cut on a sleeping animal such as a cow. Tiny heat sensors in their noses help them know where to bite. The bat then laps up blood flowing from the cut. Vampire bats are so skilled at doing this that it does not hurt the victim. Most don't even wake up.
>
> Bats need to drink about half of their body weight each night to survive. This large weight gain could make it difficult for the bats to fly. But they have adapted. The bats have developed special thumbs and strong back legs to help them get into the air.

_____

_____

_____

_____

_____

_____

_____

_____

_____

_____

SKILL 11: Identifying the Main Idea and Supporting Details

After you read, you will frequently be asked to recall or summarize the **main idea** of what you have read.

A well-written paragraph has a **main idea** and **supporting details**. The main idea is what the author is trying to say. The details provide the evidence for the main idea.

GUIDED PRACTICE

In the paragraph below, the main idea is in bold type.

> **I fell in love with Langston Terrace the very first time I saw it.** Our family had been living in two rooms of a three-story house when Mama and Daddy saw the newspaper article telling of the plans to build it. It was going to be a low-rent housing project in northeast Washington, and it would be named in honor of John Mercer Langston, the famous black lawyer, educator, and congressman.

See how a student found one supporting detail.

"It was going to be a low-rent housing project in northeast Washington"

List the other details that support the main idea.

_____
_____
_____
_____

Sometimes the main idea will be directly stated, and sometimes you will have to make a logical guess based on the details, or evidence, given in the paragraph.

> Something about my mother attracts ornithologists. It all started years ago when a couple of them discovered she had a rare species of woodpecker coming to her bird feeder. They came in the house and sat around the window, exclaiming and taking pictures with big fancy cameras. But long after the red cockaded woodpeckers had gone to roost, the ornithologists were still there. There always seemed to be three or four of them wandering around our place and staying for supper.

See how a student explained, and gave evidence, why choice "A, B, C" is correct or incorrect.

Which sentence best describes the main idea of the paragraph?
   A. A rare species of woodpecker could be found near the house.
   B. The ornithologists were excited to see the house pets.
   C. The ornithologists would sit around the window, take pictures, and then stay for supper.
   D. Something other than birds led the ornithologists to stay at the house.

A. It's true that a rare woodpecker could be found near the house. The story, however, focuses more on the reaction of the ornithologists to the woodpeckers. So this seems more like a detail than a main idea.

B. There is nothing in the paragraph that says that the ornithologists were excited to see the house pets. This answer choice is wrong.

C. Everything in this answer is in the paragraph, but the answer is a list of details, not an idea.

Now see if you can explain, and give evidence, why choice D is correct or incorrect.

D._____

_____

_____

_____

_____

NAME _____ DATE _____

NOW YOU TRY IT!

Read the paragraph. Explain, and give evidence, why each choice (A, B, C, D) is correct or incorrect.

> Once there was a woodcutter who minded everyone's business but his own. If you were digging a hole, he knew a better way to grip the shovel. If you were cooking a fish, he knew a better recipe. As his village said, he knew a little of everything and most of nothing.

Which sentence best describes the main idea of the paragraph?

A. Everyone agreed that the woodcutter was the best cook in the village.

B. The woodcutter was a foolish man who interfered in other people's business.

C. Everyone knew that the woodcutter could cut down trees better than anyone.

D. The woodcutter knew how to grip a shovel.

A. _____

_____

B. _____

_____

C. _____

_____

D. _____

_____

Skill 12: Connecting to What You Read

Making connections means to think about how what you already know is similar to what you are reading.

As you read, ask yourself, "Can I connect the passage to something I already know?" What you know can relate to any of these categories.

- your personal experience
- something you have read before
- the world

GUIDED PRACTICE

See how a student made connections between the text and what she knows.

A Coal-Powered Motorcycle?

Did you know that the motorcycle was invented before the gasoline engine? In 1869 a man named Sylvester H. Roper showed off a two-wheeled, motorized vehicle at a fair. People came from far away to see the strange machine. It looked kind of like a bicycle, but where were the pedals?

Roper showed them why it didn't need pedals. A small boiler heated up, creating steam that powered the back wheel. Like today's motorcycles, Roper's would speed up and slow down by twisting the handgrip. Roper's steam-powered motorcycle was ahead of its time. Many years would pass before motorcycles would become popular.

What connections can you make between yourself, or your life, and the passage?
Unlike Roper, I don't really know how steam-powered engines work. But Roper was interested in new things. I am also interested in new things like mp3 players.

What connections can you make between something you have read before and the passage?
I have read a lot about early cars, which were gas-powered machines that changed the way people traveled. Later motorcycles also used gas-powered engines and changed the way people traveled.

Now see if you can make the following connection.

What connections can you make between what you know about the world and the passage?

_____

_____

_____

NAME _____ DATE _____

NOW YOU TRY IT!

Read the passage below and make connections between what you already know and what you are reading, to answer the questions that follow the passage.

Swimming is Good for You

You probably already know that swimming is fun. But have you thought about the exercise that you're getting while you and your friends splash around? Swimming is one of the best ways to get exercise. When you swim, you use almost all of your muscles. Swimming is also good for your heart and lungs. Although playing in the pool will give you some exercise, swimming laps will provide the most benefit. If you decide to start an exercise program, be sure to take it slow at first. Swim for brief periods, resting between laps.

Swimming is easier on your body than many land-based kinds of exercise. Jogging, for example, is stressful to knees and ankles. It's easy to move around in the water. You weigh only about one tenth of what you weigh on land. This lighter weight is particularly helpful for people with back problems. It is also helpful for people who are trying to lose weight.

What connections can you make between yourself, or your life, and the passage?

_____

_____

_____

What connections can you make between something you have read before and the passage?

_____

_____

_____

What connections can you make between what you know about the world and the passage?

_____

_____

_____

© by Pearson Education, Inc., publishing as Pearson Prentice Hall

SKILL 13: Making Inferences from Narrative Passages

Your sister runs in the door, wearing a heavy coat and dusting snow out of her hair. You do not need your sister to tell you that it is snowing—you can make a logical guess, or **inference**, based on the information in front of you.

When we read, we make inferences to help us identify the meaning of a passage—meaning that is not spelled out on the page, but is there "between the lines."

GUIDED PRACTICE

Read the following narrative passage. Pay attention to how hints from the passage and your own experience allow you to make inferences, and learn a lot more about Lydia and her life than is actually printed on the page.

> Lydia had to be at the field in 20 minutes. This year would be different. She wouldn't mess up and end up in the stands watching the other girls score goals. Her father would be proud that she was following in Julia's footsteps. The coach would be impressed with how much Lydia had improved. All those hours of kicking the ball in the backyard with Julia, while Julia was home on break from college, would finally pay off. Lydia ran downstairs. Maybe she'd left her sneakers in the living room. Lydia's sneaker was there, torn to shreds. Dropping his tail between his legs, Spot looked up at Lydia with big eyes and whined pitifully.

Look at how one student answered a few questions about the passage by making inferences. Fill in the missing inferences.

Questions	Student Inferences
1. Why is Lydia going to the field?	She is trying out for the soccer team.
2. What happened to Lydia the year before?	
3. Who is Julia?	She is Lydia's older sister.
4. What happened to Lydia's sneakers?	

Look back at the passage. What clues answer questions 2 and 4?

2. _____

4. _____

NAME _____ DATE _____

NOW YOU TRY IT!

Read the following passage and see how much information you can infer.

> "Aren't you going to finish that ice cream, Lydia? It's your favorite." Lydia sighed and shrugged her shoulders. "No thanks, Mom. I don't feel much like eating." "I think it's just as well," said Julia. "All that time practicing can really cut into your schoolwork." Lydia picked up her backpack and headed toward the door. "I'll be back soon. I have to copy four maps of Africa from the encyclopedia and look up some facts about the Sahara Desert on the Internet. I can't wait to finish this project. Mrs. Turner thinks I'll win first prize." As Lydia closed the door behind her, her father shook his head and smiled. "That kid is going places," he said.

Using information from the passage on the previous page, hints from this text, and your own knowledge, answer the following questions.

Questions	Your Inferences
1. What is Lydia's mood at the beginning?	
2. Why does she feel this way?	
3. Where is Lydia going after dinner?	
4. What subject is her project on?	
5. What is Lydia going to do with her project?	
6. How does Lydia's father feel about her?	

1. _____

2. _____

3. _____

4. _____

5. _____

6. _____

© by Pearson Education, Inc., publishing as Pearson Prentice Hall

SKILL 14: Making Inferences from Expository Passages

You can make logical guesses based on evidence, or inferences when you read expository passages, too. To make inferences, you think about what you already know to help you learn more from a passage. Inferences allow you to gather information that is not directly stated in the passage. You make inferences when you apply what you have learned to another situation.

GUIDED PRACTICE

Read the following passage. Look and see how one student answered a few questions about the passage by making inferences. Then see which clues helped her make her inferences.

Your Hardworking Heart

Your heart is kind of like a pump. The right side of your heart receives blood from the body. It then pumps the blood to the lungs, where it is refreshed. The left side of the heart does the exact opposite. It receives blood from the lungs and pumps it out to the body. Your heart fills with blood before it beats. Then it contracts, or squeezes, to push the blood along. Your heart does this continually every day of your life.

See how the student completed the chart and then identified the clues that helped her answer the questions. **Complete the chart and identify the clues that helped you make your inference.**

Questions	Inferences
1. Why does the heart pump blood to the lungs?	The blood gets oxygen from the lungs.
2. Why does the heart contract every day of your life?	You need blood to circulate to stay alive
3. In what way is the heart like a pump?	

Which clues helped answer the questions?
1. lungs refresh blood from the body
2. the body needs fresh air, which is circulated by the heart
3. _____

NAME _____ DATE _____

NOW YOU TRY IT!

Read the following passage. Then look at how one student answered a few of the questions about the passage by making inferences.

Meteors

It's a perfect night for stargazing—dark and clear. Suddenly, a streak of light flashes across the sky. For an hour or so, you see a streak at least once a minute. You are watching a meteor shower. Meteor showers happen regularly, several times a year.

Even when there is no meteor shower, you often can see meteors if you are far from city lights and the sky is not cloudy. On average, a meteor streaks overhead every ten minutes.

A meteoroid is a chunk of rock or dust in space. Meteoroids come from comets or asteroids. Some meteroids form when asteroids collide in space. Others form when a comet breaks up and creates a cloud of dust that continues to move through the solar system. When Earth passes through one of these dust clouds, bits of dust enter Earth's atmosphere.

When a meteoroid enters Earth's atmosphere, friction with the air creates heat and produces a streak of light in the sky—a meteor. If the meteoroid is large enough, it may not burn up completely.

Use information from the passage and your own knowledge to answer the following questions.

Questions	Inferences
1. What is the difference between a meteor and a meteoroid?	
2. What is a comet?	
3. What happens if a meteoroid does not burn up completely?	

Now look back at the passage and list the clues that helped you answer the questions.

1. _____

2. _____

3. _____

© by Pearson Education, Inc., publishing as Pearson Prentice Hall

SKILL 15: MAKING PREDICTIONS

You **make predictions** when you make an informed guess about what will come next in a story or passage. It is helpful to make predictions before and while you read.

To make predictions, follow these steps as you read:
- Find clues about what might come next by looking for important details.
- Stop at different times as you read and write down your predictions.
- As you continue reading, check to see if your predictions are correct.

When your predictions are correct, you know that you understand what you are reading. When your predictions are incorrect, you can reread the passage to better understand it.

GUIDED PRACTICE

Read the first passage. Then read the chart to see how a student made a prediction and answer the question that follows.

The Giant Panda

Only about 1,000 giant pandas are left in China. Pandas live in large bamboo forests because that is what they eat. Pandas need at least two types of bamboo to survive. In the past, pandas could find food easily, but as more people move into their areas, pandas are having trouble getting enough bamboo. Their habitats, places safe for them to live, are shrinking.

Important Details	Student Prediction
rare mammal; shrinking habitat	I predict the author will write about steps being taken to help pandas

Conservation groups and Chinese officials are now working to save the pandas' habitat. A key aspect of this is the creation of bamboo "corridors" that pandas can travel through. These areas of land allow pandas to travel to other areas that have the types of bamboo the animals need.

Was the student's prediction correct? What evidence supports his prediction?

_____

_____

NAME _____ DATE _____

NOW YOU TRY IT!

Read the first paragraph of the passage below. Stop and predict what the next paragraph will be about. Then, read the rest of the passage to see if your prediction was correct. Write your answers in the chart provided. Answer the questions that follow the passage.

Skyscrapers

By the mid-1800s, American cities such as New York had grown rapidly. People from around the world were moving to the United States. As the cities grew, they spread out. Traveling from a home in the outer city to a business in the city center was becoming increasingly time-consuming. Architects tried to solve this problem by designing taller buildings so cities would not have to be so spread out. But buildings constructed with bricks or stone were very heavy. They could rise only a few stories before they would collapse.

Important Details	Your Prediction

Henry Bessemer provided the solution. He developed a method to mass produce steel. This allowed steel to be produced quickly and cheaply enough to serve as the frame for a tall structure. Steel, rather than stone or brick, would bear most of the weight of the building.

George Fuller was the first person to take advantage of steel's benefits. In 1889 his firm built the Tacoma Building in Chicago. It was the first structure in which the outer walls did not support the weight of the building. The outside of the building could have larger windows, which let in more light. Because of steel, architects could design buildings that stretched toward the sky.

What do you think will come next in the passage? What evidence supports your prediction?

_____

_____

What did you learn about skyscrapers that will help you make predictions when you read about another innovation?

_____

_____

© by Pearson Education, Inc., publishing as Pearson Prentice Hall

SKILL 16: VISUALIZING WHAT YOU READ

When you **visualize what you read**, you make a picture in your mind of what the passage describes. Visualizing makes reading more interesting. It can also help you connect what you already know to what you are reading. You can visualize by paying attention to descriptive details as you read, and use the details to spark your imagination. Remember that people visualize what they read in their own way.

GUIDED PRACTICE

Read the passage and find out how different students visualized the passage below. Then answer the questions that follow.

> Humans have found shelter in the caverns of Carlsbad National Park for more than a thousand years. Today tourists visit this natural wonder and are amazed at the jewel-like formations 900 feet underneath the deserts of New Mexico. At Carlsbad National Park, visitors can see one of the largest underground chambers in the world. This chamber, called the Big Room, is 340 feet tall. Many of the most spectacular formations are in that chamber. Both the formations and small underground pools are lit with subtle colored electric lights. Being in such an enormous space can make you feel small, even insignificant. A visit to this national treasure is a truly unique experience.

Student	Visualization
Maya	I saw huge sparkling rocks.
Trevor	I saw rocks reflected in small ponds.
Ashley	I saw an enormous cavern with lots of small people.

What did you visualize when you read this passage?

_____

_____

What key words helped the students visualize the events of this passage?

_____

_____

NAME _____ DATE _____

NOW YOU TRY IT!

Read the passage below. Get together with a small group of students. Share your visualizations with the group. Use the discussion prompts below the passage to help you.

> When you go to an amusement park, the Ferris Wheel is usually a nice relaxing ride where you can enjoy the view. You sit in a car with two or four people and are gently lifted up and around. At the top, you look out and see the tops of trees, ant-like people, and a sea of cars in the parking lot.
>
> The experience of the passengers on the first Ferris Wheel was much more of an adventure. Built in 1893 for the World Columbian Exposition in Chicago by George W. G. Ferris, the spider-web-like steel frame had a maximum height of 264 feet. There were 36 wooden cars and each car held 60 people. The best time to ride the Ferris Wheel was when the sun set, and the orange and purple haze streaked across the sky. When passengers reached the top of the Wheel they were four stories taller than the tallest building in Chicago at that time.

What picture came to mind first?

_____

_____

What key words helped you visualize?

_____

_____

What prior experience helped you visualize?

_____

_____

How are other students' visualizations similar to or different from yours?

_____

_____

On a separate piece of paper, draw a picture of something described in the passage.

© by Pearson Education, Inc., publishing as Pearson Prentice Hall

TEST PREP

Directions: Use the During Reading Strategies you learned to help you understand the passage below. Be on the look out for important characters, events, and details. Remember that the indented words summarize the passage events and details and the author's actual words are not indented.

The All-American Slurp
by Lensey Namioka

Introduction: In this story a Chinese family must deal with unfamiliar American eating habits. The following are some Chinese meal-time customs. Tea is usually served during or after meals. Food is usually served "family style" on large platters in the center of the table. The only individual dishes are rice bowls. And, food is eaten with slender sticks called chopsticks.

"As any respectable Chinese knows, the correct way to eat your soup is to <u>slurp</u>."

The first time our family was invited out to dinner in America, we disgraced ourselves while eating celery. We had <u>emigrated</u> to this country from China, and during our early days here we had a hard time with American table manners.

◆ ◆ ◆

> The Lins had never eaten raw vegetables in China. They had always cleaned their vegetables in boiling water. Seeing raw celery on a relish tray surprises them.
>
> The Lins are invited to dinner at the home of their neighbors, the Gleasons. When the Lins arrive, the friends shake hands and the Lin family sits on the sofa.
>
> When Mrs. Gleason offers them the relish tray, the Lins each take a piece of celery. They are surprised by how good it tastes. However, the celery strings get caught in the narrator's teeth, so she pulls them out of the celery. Her brother and her parents do the same.

◆ ◆ ◆

Suddenly I realized that there was dead silence... Looking up, I saw that the eyes of everyone in the room were on our family. Mr. and Mrs. Gleason, their daughter Meg, who was my friend, and their neighbors the Badels—they were all staring at us as we busily pulled the strings of our celery...

◆ ◆ ◆

VOCABULARY

slurp (SLERP)
v. sip loudly

emigrated
(em I GRAYT id)
v. left one country to settle in another

48   © by Pearson Education, Inc., publishing as Pearson Prentice Hall

When the narrator sees her friend Meg the next day, she doesn't know if they will still be friends. But Meg acts the same as usual, and the narrator begins to relax. Meg was the narrator's first friend in America and is still her only real friend.

❖ ❖ ❖

My brother didn't have any problems making friends. He spent all his time with some boys who were teaching him baseball, and in no time he could speak English much faster than I could—not better, but faster.

I worried more about making mistakes, and I spoke carefully, making sure I could say everything right before opening my mouth.

❖ ❖ ❖

The narrator also worries about her appearance. She wants to wear blue jeans to school, but her mother insists she wear skirts.

❖ ❖ ❖

By the time she saw that Meg and the other girls were wearing jeans, it was too late. My school clothes were bought already, and we didn't have money left to buy new outfits for me. We had too many other things to buy first, like furniture, pots, and pans. . .

❖ ❖ ❖

At the end of the month, the narrator's mother buys her some blue jeans. Other family members make important changes as well. Her brother makes his school baseball team, her father begins driving lessons, and her mother discovers <u>rummage sales</u>.

❖ ❖ ❖

We soon got all the furniture we needed, plus a dart board and a 1,000-piece jigsaw puzzle. . . There was hope that the Lins might become a normal American family after all.

Then came our dinner at the Lakeview restaurant.

The Lakeview was an expensive restaurant, one of those places where a headwaiter dressed in <u>tails</u> conducted you to your seat, and the only light came from candles and flaming desserts. In one corner of the room a lady harpist played tinkling melodies.

❖ ❖ ❖

The Lins have trouble reading their menus, which are written in French. They decide to order their meals at random. When the soup arrives in a plate, they are unsure of how to eat it.

❖ ❖ ❖

> **VOCABULARY**
>
> **rummage sale**
> (RUM ij SAYL)
> *v.* a sale of used household items
>
> **tails** (TAYLZ) *n.* a man's formal evening suit

Fortunately my parents had studied books on western <u>etiquette</u> before they came to America. "Tilt your plate," whispered my mother. "It's easier to spoon the soup up that way."

She was right. Tilting the plate did the trick. But the etiquette book didn't say anything about what you did after the soup reached your lips. As any respectable Chinese knows, the correct way to eat your soup is to slurp. This helps to cool the liquid and prevent you from burning your lips. It also shows your appreciation.

We showed our appreciation. Shloop, went my father. Shloop went my mother. Shloop, shloop, went my brother, who was the hungriest.

The lady harpist stopped playing to take a rest. And in the silence, our family's <u>consumption</u> of soup suddenly seemed unnaturally loud.

◆ ◆ ◆

> At the sound of the slurping, the waiter freezes, and so does the nearby diners. Humiliated, the narrator jumps up and runs to the bathroom. She stays there for the rest of the meal.

◆ ◆ ◆

But by the time we had been in this country for three months, our family was definitely making progress toward becoming Americanized...

The day came when my parents announced that they wanted to give a dinner party. We had invited Chinese friends to eat with us before, but this dinner was going to be different. In addition to a Chinese-American family, we were going to invite the Gleasons.

◆ ◆ ◆

> Normally, the Lins eat from platters set in the middle of the table. They use chopsticks to bring food from the platters to their rice bowls. This time, they set their table with large American dinner plates. During dinner the narrator is shocked when her friend Meg mixes all the different foods on her plate. It is a Chinese tradition to finish eating food taken from one dish before taking food from another.

◆ ◆ ◆

I couldn't bear to look any longer, and I turned to Mr. Gleason. He was chasing a pea around his plate. Several times he got it to the edge, but when he tried to pick it up with his chopsticks, it rolled back toward the center of the plate again. Finally he put down his chopsticks and picked up the pea with his fingers. He really did! A grown man!

◆ ◆ ◆

VOCABULARY

etiquette (ET I ket) *n.* acceptable social manners

comsumption (kuhn SUMP shuhn) *n.* eating; drinking; using up

The narrator wants to laugh as she and the Chinese guests watch the Gleasons eat. But a look from her mother makes her realize that the Gleasons are not used to Chinese ways. It makes the narrator think of celery strings.

After dinner, Meg decides she wants a big chocolate milkshake. She convinces her friend, the narrator, to walk with her to the ice cream shop.

◆ ◆ ◆

Toward the end she pulled hard on her straws and went shloop, shloop.

"Do you always slurp when you eat a milkshake?" I asked, before I could stop myself.

Meg grinned. "Sure. All Americans slurp."

Answer the questions below.

1. In the first paragraph, you learn that
   A. the narrator's family emigrated from China.
   B. the narrator was unsure of how to use a fork.
   C. the narrator likes to drink milkshakes.
   D. the narrator's family likes to eat celery.

2. In paragraph three, stole means
   F. to have taken property without permission.
   G. a kind of fur worn on the shoulders.
   H. to have taken or done secretly.
   J. to have given something away.

3. The sequence of events of the plot is
   A. Lins eat at a restaurant, narrator drinks a milkshake.
   B. Lins eat at the Gleasons, narrator gets blue jeans, Lins eat at a restaurant.
   C. narrator get blue jeans, Lins eat at a restaurant, Lins eat at the Gleasons.
   D. narrator drinks a milkshake, narrator gets blue jeans, Lins eat at a restaurant.

4. At the ice cream shop, the narrator learns that
   F. Meg likes vanilla milkshakes most.
   G. milkshakes are expensive.
   H. it is okay to slurp a milkshake.
   J. she dislikes chocolate milkshakes.

5. The narrator is best described as
   A. modest and independent.
   B. mean and smart.
   C. loud and confused.
   D. worried and anxious.

6. What will happen next in the story?
   F. Meg and the narrator will never see each other again.
   G. The narrator's family will probably move back to China.
   H. The friendship between Meg and the narrator will grow.
   J. The Gleasons will refuse to eat Chinese food again.

Something Different...
IN AND OUT OF CONTEXT

Have you ever heard only part of a conversation, and it sounded really strange? Then after asking a few questions, it didn't seem strange at all. Many misunderstandings happen when things are heard or read out of context.

Work in groups and read the sentence fragments below. Then make inferences to put each fragment in a logical context. First look for clues in the fragment. Next think about what you already know and make a logical guess.

Read the example below. Notice how the student used the clue "candy" in the fragment to infer that the fragment wasn't actually about a cat, but probably a piñata shaped like a cat.

Fragment: . . . the cat's head burst and candy fell to the ground!

Context: At my birthday party, my parents got me a piñata shaped like a cat. After many tries at bat, finally the cat's head burst and candy fell to the ground!

Fragment: . . . my brother's glow in the dark fangs.

Context: _____

_____

Fragment: . . . stopped so suddenly, I thought I might fall out of the teacup.

Context: _____

_____

Fragment: . . . third ring was just full of clowns.

Context: _____

_____

NAME _____ DATE _____

SCANNING A PASSAGE

Scanning is moving your eyes quickly down a page to find a specific piece of information. Scanning helps when you have questions about a passage.

Here's how to scan. Identify the key word(s) to search for. Scan the passage, stopping only when you find the key word(s). Read to see if the surrounding information is what you are looking for.

GUIDED PRACTICE

Here is an example of how a student used scanning to answer a question.

Read the question. The highlighted text imitates the experience of scanning for the key word(s).

What are the key word(s) to search for in the reading?

The key words in the question are Fates and thread.

What did the thread of the Fates represent?
- **A.** The relationship between the sisters
- **B.** Death
- **C.** A person's lifetime
- **D.** Their power

> Themis, the goddess of necessity, had three daughters, known as the Fates. These three supervised fate in Greek mythology. Their names are Koltho, Lakhesis, and Atropos. Klotho spun the thread of life, and Lakhesis determined the length of the thread. Atropos cut the thread when life came to an end.

Read to see if the surrounding information answers the question. Write the answer below.

_____

What did Lakhesis determine? What are the key words to search for?

_____

_____

© by Pearson Education, Inc., publishing as Pearson Prentice Hall

NOW YOU TRY IT!

First read the question. What are the key word(s) to search for?

_____

Why did the mouse help the lion?
- **A.** He was afraid of the lion.
- **B.** The lion promised not to eat him.
- **C.** The lion had let him go earlier.
- **D.** Mice often help lions.

Now scan this passage to quickly find the answer.

The Lion and the Mouse
by Aesop

Once, when a Lion was asleep, a little Mouse began running up and down upon him; this soon wakened the Lion, who placed his huge paw upon him, and opened his big jaws to swallow him. "Pardon, O King," cried the little Mouse: "forgive me this time. I shall never forget it: who knows but what I may be able to do you a turn some of these days?" The Lion was so tickled at the idea of the Mouse being able to help him that he lifted up his paw and let him go. Some time after, the Lion was caught in a trap, and the hunters, who desired to carry him alive to the King, tied him to a tree while they went in search of a wagon to carry him on. Just then the little Mouse happened to pass by, and seeing the sad plight in which the Lion was, went up to him and soon gnawed away the ropes that bound the King of the Beasts. "Was I not right?" said the little Mouse.

Little friends may prove great friends.

Read to see if the surrounding information answers the question. Write the answer below.

_____

_____

_____

_____

NAME _____ DATE _____

SKILL 18 — SUMMARIZING

To **summarize** a passage, pick out the most important ideas or events and retell them in your own words. This summary is very short. It is important to **paraphrase** (or use your own words) when you summarize, because it helps you to check your understanding. If you have difficulty summarizing a passage, you may want to reread it.

GUIDED PRACTICE

See how one student used a graphic organizer to help summarize a passage. Read the summary and the passage to fill in two important ideas.

Important Ideas
- The eruption occurred as a huge explosion.
- _____
- Giant tidal waves swamped surrounding coastal areas
- _____

→

Summary
In August, 1883, Krakatau erupted. The eruption was the most violent in modern history. At least 36,000 people lost their lives.

The Eruption of Krakatau

After years of silence, an island volcano named Krakatau in southeastern Asia sprang to life in August of 1883. It began by rumbling and spitting ash and smoke. People living near the island began to worry as the ground shook. Then suddenly the island didn't just erupt—it exploded. The sound was so loud that people could hear it thousands of miles away. Much of the island was blown to bits. After the eruption, only one third of the island remained above sea level.

The eruption caused huge, 100-foot tidal waves. Blocks of coral, weighing hundreds of tons, were thrown onto nearby lands. More than 150 coastal villages disappeared under the waves. At least 36,000 people lost their lives, mostly from the giant waves. The eruption was the most violent and deadly one of modern times.

The ash tossed up by the explosion circled the world. In some areas it made the sun look green or blue. As the ash rose higher, it caused vivid red sunsets. So red, in fact, that people in some cities called the fire department because they thought that part of the city was on fire.

© by Pearson Education, Inc., publishing as Pearson Prentice Hall

NOW YOU TRY IT!

Read the passage then complete the graphic organizer below to write a summary.

Grizzly Bears

Imagine that it's 1804. You're traveling through what will become the western part of the United States with the explorers Lewis and Clark. All the members of the group are skilled hunters. Even so, you're a little worried about a bear that some Native Americans have warned you about. They say that it's huge—and fast.

The bear that the Native Americans warned Lewis and Clark about was the grizzly, or brown, bear. The members of the expedition were used to hunting the smaller black bear. The size and speed of the grizzly bear led to some close—and frightening—encounters between man and bear.

Grizzly bears live in Alaska, Canada, and the mountains of the American West. Grizzlies that live along coastal are called brown bears, and grow larger because of richer diets. They sometimes grow to more than 1,000 pounds, while bears in the mountains can only grow to 300 pounds. The name *grizzlies* refers to the white-tipped fur that many of them possess, and which gives them a "grizzled" appearance.

Important Ideas	→	Summary
_____		_____
_____		_____
_____		_____
_____		_____
_____		_____
_____		_____
_____		_____
_____		_____
_____		_____
_____		_____

NAME _____ DATE _____

Asking Questions

Asking questions is the practice of thinking about what you want to find out from the passage as you read. Good readers ask questions before, during, and after they read. Thinking of good questions will help you recognize whether or not a passage makes sense. A good question, is a question about an important fact or detail that will probably be answered by reading the passage. You will find that asking questions will help you solve problems and find information quickly.

GUIDED PRACTICE

Use the graphic organizer to help you practice asking questions.

- First, write down what you already know about the topic.
- Begin reading the passage, then stop and decide what you want to know.
- Finally, write down the answers to your questions as you read.

Writing down the answers will show what you learned and tell you if you thought of good questions.

See how one student began to fill in the graphic organizer. **Read the passage to complete it.**

What You Know	What You Want to Know	What You Learned
The bridge is in San Francisco.	How big is the bridge?	

Building the Golden Gate Bridge

On May 27, 1937, some 200,000 people from San Francisco gathered to celebrate an amazing achievement. The Golden Gate Bridge had just been completed ahead of schedule and under budget. The span between the two towers of the bridge was the longest in the world.

Construction began in January of 1933. The workers erected two tall towers. They added two strong cables on top of the towers to support the roadway below. The bridge is almost two miles long.

NOW YOU TRY IT!

Complete the graphic organizer below to help you think of questions. Remember to first write what you know about "Fleet" Walker in the first column and then begin reading. Pause after the third sentence of the passage and think of a few questions. Write your questions in the second column. As you read, write the answers to your questions in the third column.

Moses Fleetwood "Fleet" Walker

In 1883 an African American baseball player joined the Toledo Blue Stockings. The next year, the Blue Stockings became part of the major leagues. The player, Moses Fleetwood "Fleet" Walker, at that point became the first African American major league baseball player.

Other African Americans followed Walker into the major leagues. Over the next few years, however, opposition to African American players in the major leagues grew. By 1889, Walker was once again the only major league African American player. 1889 would be his last year to play. With Walker gone, team owners and players agreed to keep African Americans out of baseball. Walker would be the last African American to play for more than 50 years, until Jackie Robinson joined the Brooklyn Dodgers.

What You Know	What You Want to Know	What You Learned

DRAWING CONCLUSIONS

You **draw conclusions** when you read by making a logical decision or a reasonable judgment. You also draw conclusions by forming a reasonable opinion. Conclusions should be based on the facts or details in a passage. People draw conclusions everyday without realizing it. For example, if a friend told you that he or she enjoys camping because of the beautiful scenery, you might draw the conclusions that your friend likes nature and being outdoors.

GUIDED PRACTICE

Below is a graphic organizer that shows how a student drew a conclusion from the passage. The student thought about two ideas and formed a reasonable opinion about the character, Jennifer. **Read the passage and see if you can draw a conclusion about the plot**. Use the graphic organizer to help you.

First Chair

   Jennifer moved her fingers silently over the flute. Long ago she had memorized the song that she hoped would help her become first chair in the band. Jennifer had practiced for weeks. "You're a different player now," her father had told her. "You should try for first chair."
   Jennifer listened as Kathy, the current first chair, played. "She's good," thought Jennifer, "but she's not perfect." When Kathy finished, she nodded at the director and hurried off the stage. Jennifer walked on the stage, smiled at the director, and started to play.

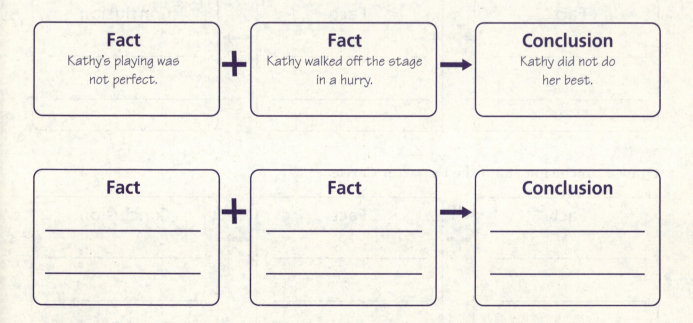

NOW YOU TRY IT!

Read the passage and draw your own conclusions by answering the questions that follow the passage.

Back to the Stable

Jimmy and Kristen struggled to carry the saddles to the stables. It was finally warm enough to ride, and they were eager to get going. They also wanted to find a horse that would be good for Carrie.

Jimmy pulled on the creaky door to the stable. Inside, they could see Stan, the stable owner. "Jimmy! Kristen!" he yelled. They were glad to see Stan. He had taught them everything they knew about riding.

"Look," Stan said, gesturing toward some horses. "We have some new friends this year."

"That's great Stan, because we have a new friend, too!" Kristen responded.

Draw a conclusion about what time of year the story takes place.

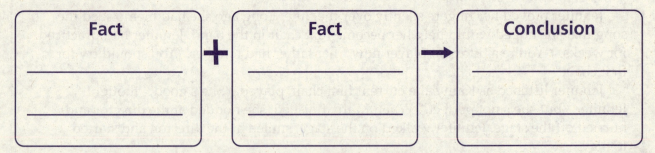

Draw a conclusion about what Jimmy and Kristen are looking for.

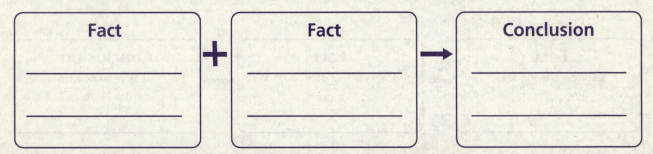

Draw a conclusion about the character Carrie.

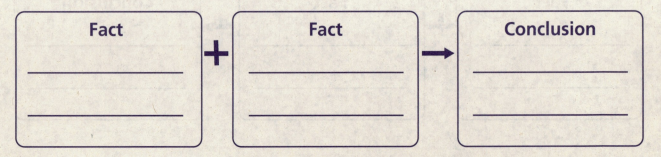

Test Prep

Directions: Use the Post-Reading strategies you learned to help you understand the passage below. Be an active reader by pausing and thinking about what you are reading as you go. Don't forget to use the skill, "Scanning the Text" to answer the questions below. Remember that the indented words summarize the passage events and details and the author's actual words are not indented.

The Wounded Wolf
by Jean Craighead George

Introduction: *This story is based on an incident the author heard of from a scientist. In retelling it, she leaves out any trace of human observation.*

A wounded wolf climbs Toklat Ridge, a <u>massive</u> spine of rock and ice. As he limps, dawn strikes the ridge and lights it up with sparks and stars. Roko, the wounded wolf, blinks in the ice fire, then stops to rest and watch his pack run the thawing Arctic valley.

They plunge and turn. They fight the mighty caribou that struck young Roko with his hoof and wounded him. He jumped between the beast and Kiglo, leader of the Toklat pack. Young Roko spun and fell. Hooves, paws, and teeth roared over him. And then his pack and the beast were gone.

<u>Gravely</u> injured, Roko pulls himself toward the shelter rock. Weakness overcomes him. He stops. He and his pack are thin and hungry. This is the season of starvation. . . .

Young Roko glances down the valley. He droops his head and stiffens his tail to signal to his pack that he is badly hurt. Winds <u>wail</u>. A frigid blast picks up long <u>shawls</u> of snow and drapes them between young Roko and his pack. And so his message is not read.

❖❖❖

   A nearby raven sees Roko's signal and calls out that something is dying. Soon Roko is followed by a group of hungry ravens.

❖❖❖

Roko snarls and hurries toward the shelter rock. A cloud of snow envelops him. He limps in blinding whiteness now.

A ghostly presence flits around. "Hahahahahahaha," the white fox states—death is coming to the Ridge. Roko smells the fox tagging at his heels.

The cloud whirls off. Two golden eyes look up at Roko. The snowy owl has heard the ravens and joined the deathwatch.

❖❖❖

   The ravens, fox, and owl are joined by a grizzly bear. The animals follow Roko as he struggles up Toklat Ridge. As Roko becomes weaker, the other animals grow bold and move in closer.

VOCABULARY

massive (MAS iv)
adj. huge; large and impressive

gravely (GRAYV lee)
adv. badly

wail (WAYL)
v. make a loud crying sound

shawl (SHAWL)
n. cape-like cloth

Roko stops; his breath comes hard. A raven <u>alights</u> upon his back and picks the open wound. Roko snaps. The raven flies and circles back. The white fox nips at Roko's toes. The snowy owl inches closer. The grizzly bear, still dulled by sleep, stumbles onto Toklat Ridge.

Only yards from the shelter rock, Roko falls. Instantly the ravens mob him. They scream and peck and stab at his eyes. The white fox leaps upon his wound. The snowy owl sits and waits.

Young Roko struggles to his feet. He bites the ravens. Snaps the fox. And lunges at the <u>stoic</u> owl. He turns and warns the grizzly bear. Then he bursts into a run and falls against the shelter rock. The wounded wolf wedges down between the rock and <u>barren</u> ground. Now protected on three sides, he turns and faces all his foes.

The ravens step a few feet closer. The fox slides toward him on his belly. The snowy owl blinks and waits, and on the ridge rim roars the hungry grizzly bear.

Roko growls.

The sun comes up. Far across the Toklat Valley, Roko hears his pack's "hunt's end" song. The music wails and sobs, wilder than the bleating wind. The hunt song ends. Next comes the roll call. Each member of the Toklat pack barks to say that he is home and well.

"Kiglo here," Roko hears his leader bark. There is a pause. It is young Roko's turn. He cannot lift his head to answer. The pack is silent. The leader starts the count once more. "Kiglo here."—A pause. Roko cannot answer.

❖ ❖ ❖

> Soon Kiglo hears the ravens' death song. He knows that Roko is dying.

❖ ❖ ❖

The hours pass. The wind slams snow on Toklat Ridge. Massive clouds blot out the sun. In their gloom Roko sees the deathwatch move in closer. Suddenly he hears the musk-oxen thundering into their circle. The ice cracks as the grizzly leaves. The ravens burst into the air. The white fox runs. The snowy owl flaps to the top of the shelter rock. And Kiglo rounds the <u>knoll</u>.

In his mouth he carries meat. He drops it close to Roko's head and wags his tail excitedly. Roko licks Kiglo's chin to honor him. Then Kiglo puts his mouth around Roko's nose. This gesture says "I am your leader." . . .

The wounded wolf wags his tail. Kiglo trots away.

Already Roko's wound feels better. . . .

❖ ❖ ❖

> Kiglo continues to bring food to Roko. Each day, Roko grows stronger.

❖ ❖ ❖

VOCABULARY

alights (uh LIYTS)
v. lands

stoic (STO ik)
adj. showing no reaction to good or bad events; calm and unaffected by hardship

barren (BAR en)
adj. empty

knoll (NOHL)
n. hill

One dawn he moves his wounded leg. He stretches it and pulls himself into the sunlight. He walks—he romps. He runs in circles. He leaps and plays with chunks of ice. Suddenly he stops. The "hunt's end" song rings out. Next comes the roll call.

"Kiglo here."

"Roko here," he barks out strongly.

The pack is silent.

"Kiglo here," the leader repeats.

"Roko here."

Across the distance comes the sound of whoops and yipes and barks and howls. They fill the dawn with celebration. And Roko prances down the Ridge.

Answer the questions below.

1. **Which of the following facts should be included in a summary?**
   A. Wolves eat caribou.
   B. Ravens pecked at Roko's eyes.
   C. Roko was injured while hunting.
   D. Roko signaled he was sick by drooping his head.

2. **What do Kiglo's actions indicate about wolves?**
   F. they they kill wounded wolves
   G. that they are poor hunters
   H. that they help and protect one another
   J. all of the above

3. **The relationship between Kiglo and Roko is important because**
   A. Roko depended upon Kiglo for survival.
   B. It demonstrates the close relationships between wolves.
   C. Kiglo was determined to remain the leader of the wolves.
   D. Kiglo could drive away the other animals.

4. **Why do you think Roko was wounded?**
   F. He is a young wolf who probably has less experience hunting than the others.
   G. He was probably trying to impress Kiglo by being especially aggressive.
   H. The caribou probably knew that Roko could be easily wounded.
   J. He might have already been hurt, which made him easier to be wounded again.

5. **What questions do you have that were not answered in the passage? Explain how you would find the answers to your questions.**

_____

_____

Something Different...
Putting Two and Two Together

The phrase "putting two and two together" means to make a logical connection between two facts. Many times the result of putting two and two together is a conclusion.

Read the facts below. Write the facts on separate pieces of paper. Fold each paper in four and put them into a hat (or box). Take turns drawing one fact from the hat, and reading it aloud to the class. As you listen to your classmates' facts, try to make a connection between your fact and the fact being read. Remember which classmate has a fact that you can connect to your fact. After all of the facts are read, pair up with the classmate you remembered. Work together to draw as many conclusions as you can from the two facts. Write your conclusions on a separate piece of paper.

Facts

1. **Many types of female bats group together to make a nursery before they have their babies. They usually make their nurseries in a cave.**

2. **Many types of bears are omnivores. They eat grubs, berries and herbaceous plants in huge quantities. They also eat squirrels, mice, and fish.**

3. *Vertebrates* are either *cold-blooded* or *warm-blooded*. **A vertebrate is cold-blooded if the temperature inside its body is the same as the temperature outside of it.**

4. **The home of many White Tail deer is the deciduous forests. They are mostly active at night, but they can be active at any time.**

5. **A *deciduous forest* is a kind of biome. *Deciduous* means "to fall off or shed."**

6. **A *troglobiont* is an organism that lives in a cave.**

7. **The desert iguana can change its color from gray to almost pure white, in order to control its body temperature. It turns white to reflect the sunlight and stop from becoming too hot.**

8. **The blue jay is omnivorous. Many live in deciduous forests.**